My Days of Sorrow
and Joy
in Rwanda

Betsy Kain

Cover design by Nancy Smith. Text layout by Craig Smith and Nancy Winter.

Published and distributed by IngramSpark under their imprint Indy Pub.

ISBN: 978-1-0879-4129-5

A compelling and absorbing book by an incredible lady about her work with the survivors of the 1994 genocide in Rwanda. Marvel at her unending fund raising efforts to buy goats and cows for the survivors. A vivid description of a people with great needs and amazing resilience and courage.

Dedication

This book is written in honor of B. Justin Bisengimana. He has spent more than 15 years dedicated to improving the lives of thousands of Rwandans. His persistence in the face of many obstacles has made our Rwanda project a success. We will always be very grateful to him. And for the courageous, brave survivors of the 1994 genocide.

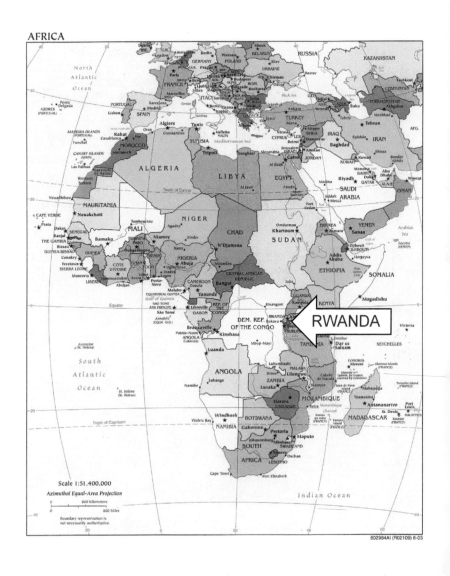

United States Central Intelligence Agency. *Africa*. [Washington, D.C.: Central Intelligence Agency, 1981] Map. https://www.loc.gov/item/97687550/.

Contents

1

Introduction

Rwanda is an interesting country, only the size of Maryland but with a population of 12.6 million. The capital city of Kigali has a population of 1.2 million. 90% of the people live by subsistence farming; cash crops are mainly coffee and tea. Women hold 61% of the seats in parliament.

Most tourists come to see the gorillas first and then they come down to Kigali just for one or two nights to see the museums about the 1994 genocide. There is also a wild animal park outside the city. It has been enlarged considerably in recent years. Many animals were killed for food during the genocide.

Rwanda is mountainous, especially in the northern part of the country, where the gorillas reside. Lake Kivu, one of the largest lakes in Africa, is located on the western edge of Rwanda. The hills are rolling and beautiful. In my many trips, the people were very welcoming and happy to see us.

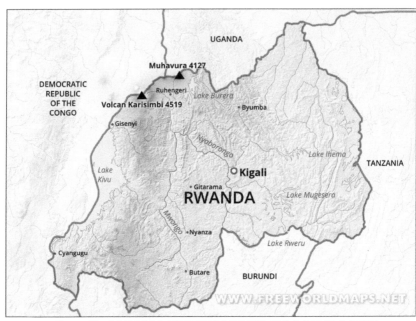

Credit: WWW.FREEWORLDMAPS.NET

People often ask me if it is safe to travel in Rwanda. In general, I felt safe. Only on one occasion did I feel insecure. Dusk had arrived and I had just missed the hourly bus to my destination. A Rwandan man across the street had been observing me standing at the bus stop. Eventually he crossed the street and said to me, in perfect English, "You have been here for a long time in the hot sun. You don't look like a typical tourist." I replied, "Yes, and I am getting worried, because it is getting dark." We struck up a conversation about what I was doing in Rwanda. When the next terribly crowded bus for my destination arrived, he pushed onto the bus. He must have explained that I was here doing humanitarian work and asked if anyone would be willing to get off the bus so that I could get home before dark. Picture the situation: a bus crowded with Rwandans who were also trying to get home after a day of work were asked to give up a seat to some well-to-do foreigner. Almost immediately a middle-aged Rwandan woman stepped out of the bus holding two bags, probably containing dinner for her family. She would now have to wait for at least another hour for the next bus that might not have room for her. I said, "Murakoze, murakoze (Thank you, thank you)!" I got home safely in the dark.

Rwanda has suffered from European colonial expansion in the 19th century and then from the terrible 1994 genocide. Hutu militias, armed primarily with machetes, slaughtered one million Tutsis (or Tutsi sympathizers). Women (more than an estimated 250,000) were sometimes raped before being killed or turned into sex slaves; the Tutsi male population was decimated. There were courageous Hutus and Muslims who risked their lives by hiding terrified Tutsis from the murderous militias. Still more than 33,000 Rwandans died every day during the genocide. Meanwhile, western nations were aware this was occurring, but did little to stop it.

In fact, prior to the 1994 genocide, the French not only helped the Hutus purchase the machetes, but also demonstrated how to kill more efficiently. An aid worker who had lived through the genocide told me he had observed French soldiers teaching Hutus how to most efficiently kill someone with a machete. They used live goats for the demonstration.

Grandparents' house in Senatobia, MS

2

Background for My Work in Rwanda

I now realize that much of my earlier life had prepared me for my work in Rwanda. In particular, I remember my many happy visits to my grandparents in Senatobia, MS, and my education and career as a clinical social worker. While in Senatobia, my brother Charles and I most enjoyed playing with Shirley and Frank. They were poor blacks who lived down a dirt road from my grandparents' house. We always enjoyed being with them and looked forward to many playtimes together.

Shirley and Frank with Charles

I was always very concerned when I would go with my granddaddy to visit the tenant farmers. They were always very friendly. They liked Mr Gabbert, as they called him. I was assured that my granddaddy treated them with respect and would even pay for their medical treatment in Memphis, if necessary.

Tenant Farmers

Their living conditions, however, were quite poor. There was no denying that there was an enormous difference in living standards between black and white communities.

My father became the Presbyterian minister in Eufaula, Alabama. Daddy would sometimes be invited to preach on Sunday afternoons or evenings at the black church when their black preacher was not available. He enjoyed this opportunity. He would also drive with me to the black section of town to pick up the ironing from a very sweet black woman. My father had received his theological education at Union Seminary in New York City which was very liberal. (While he was at the seminary, Dietrich Bonhoeffer was teaching there. The famous German theologian and anti-Nazi was appalled at the way New Yorkers treated blacks, according to my mother.) From Eufaula we moved to New Orleans in 1956. Only when I was in college did I learn from a Eufaula friend the real reason we moved away from Eufaula. The people in the congregation were uncomfortable with daddy's affinity with black people.

Perhaps these experiences in Senatobia and with my father over many years led me to feel at home in Rwanda — with its very red dirt and hot weather and the very friendly black people.

A second factor that preconditioned me to agree to work in Rwanda was my training in clinical social work, a master's degree in social work at Richmond Professional Institute in Richmond, VA. My second-year training placement was in a psychiatric out-patient agency for troubled children and parents. My first job out of graduate school was in inpatient psychiatry at the University of Michigan psychiatric hospital. After my husband and I moved to Pittsburgh, PA, I started working at another child-guidance center with the University of Pittsburgh. This training gave me the courage to undertake working with traumatized survivors of the 1994 genocide in Rwanda.

3

Becoming Involved with Rwanda: The Tinsleys

I became involved with Rwanda through a wonderful British couple living part-time in Santa Barbara, Henry and Rebecca Tinsley, who were concerned about human rights. They had visited Rwanda several times and observed the physical and emotional effects on the survivors of the 1994 genocide. One Sunday after church they asked me if I had any ideas about how they might help these distraught, traumatized people. I started to give them just the simplest sorts of relaxation techniques, such as tapping (where you tap on pressure points) and of course deep breathing. Several weeks later, Rebecca told me that Henry and she had decided that I should go to Rwanda to teach these methods. They also suggested that David come along to help Rebecca's other project: building a girl's school for poor girls who had the potential to be future leaders. At that time, the only school was limited to wealthier families.

David and I had taken another trip to South Africa six months earlier to help at an orphanage for AIDS survivors. I was surprised that we would travel to Africa so soon again. Rebecca, however, was (and still is) very persuasive. They would even pay for most of our expenses. They felt our help would be very useful.

Rebecca Tinsley   Betsy and David Kain
(Right photo courtesy of Paul Wellman)

Others heard about our plans. Most lived in Santa Barbara. Therefore, the initial planning meetings were held in our home. We also met in London on our way to Rwanda. These meetings had two goals: meet non-Californians who would be on the trip and finalize the Rwandan itinerary. We accepted the Tinsley's generous offer to stay in their home for three nights.

We were not surprised by our initial impressions of this country: beautiful hills but unbelievable poverty. We saw the gorillas, a wonderful, though expensive adventure; we visited the beautiful national park where the giraffes, hippos, zebras, and other wild animals could roam freely.

Traveling to these destinations could not be done without noticing their poverty. After seeing the gorillas, we drove through local villages near the gorilla site. We saw up close the extreme poverty: as many as six people live in these shabby structures.

One situation was sadly very common. A woman was comforting her husband who was dying of AIDS. She also had a baby, but virtually no shelter, a few twigs and branches to give them some shade, but little protection from rain or cold weather.

On a later trip, I stopped by a Roman Catholic confine where our leader knew the priest. They had known each other for years and were very happy to see each other. We were invited in to have lunch with him. What moved me was the sight of a very young girl, perhaps six or seven years old but who did not speak. She grabbed my hand and showed me around the area. She made it very clear she wanted me to take her photo. She climbed up a nearby tree and smiled sweetly. Obviously, she had been photographed before.

A nun who lived there told us that this child had apparently been abandoned. She had no parents and was walking alone down a road. They picked her up and brought her into the parsonage to treat her wounds. They also gave her food and shelter. The girl was unable to speak, although you could feel she wanted to communicate. The nun explained that she had never talked. One can only guess how she had been terribly traumatized. I shall always remember her engaging smile and warmth.

$\boxed{4}$

Justin Bisengimana: Rwanda Program Director

(Photos courtesy of World Dance for Humanity)

(Photo courtesy of Harriet Eckstein)

Justin is the most remarkable human being I have ever met. He worked at the guesthouse where we stayed on my first trip to Rwanda. He responded to and completed every request a guest would have. This included carrying the suitcases up to your room, repairing toilets, and any repairs around the guesthouse. He was a delightful person with excellent English, a perfect intro-duction to Rwanda for us.

Later I asked how his English was so good. He said it was because he spent years in a refugee camp in Uganda. I also asked why he was so compassionate and eager to help people. He responded that his mother told him you must always help other people.

In the beginning David and I knew that we wanted to work with these survivors. Clearly we needed somebody to translate for us. We did not speak Kinyarwanden. Justin did an admirable job translating. Fortunately, he had gotten several degrees from his university studies, including a master's degree in project management, specializing in non-government agencies (NGOs). This degree would be very valuable for our work.

When we went out into the country, Justin usually contacted in advance people in the villages with the greatest need. If they did not have a phone, we would simply go there. He would explain why I was there with him.

White people were quite a curiosity when we went out into the country. In Rwanda parents told children that if they misbehave a mazunga (a white person) would come and get them and take them away. Some communities had never seen a white person. When we first went into a village, often very young children would be quite frightened and cling to their mother's leg or hide their face in her dress. Older children knew better, and they would come up and very shyly touch me just with a finger to feel this white skin and then run away, giggling.

I could better understand Justin's admirable qualities after meeting his mother Julian, quiet but very committed to helping others, especially children. For instance, not many people would assume responsibility for an abandon baby. She already had assumed care for several abandoned children. One baby had been left on the sidewalk wrapped in a blanket. She took the child to the police station. They had no idea who the parents were. She felt she had to bring the baby to her home. This baby is now a very beautiful girl. Today she has now assumed responsibility for seven children despite a very limited income.

Julian and Justin
(Photo courtesy of World Dance for Humanity)

In addition, the houses she could only afford to rent to live in were very poorly built, making them vulnerable when heavy rains came each April. As a result, she had to undertake frequent moves with her large extended family. In her case, we knew a compassionate American donor who offered to build her a more substantial house. I stayed two nights at the new home, which was comfortable and safe. This is a HOME, not an orphanage! In addition, the donor gave money for farmland for livestock and vegetables nearby.

She has a Rwandan name but for Americans like me she is simply called Mama. Unfortunately, she does have a number of medical issues including high blood pressure. She is taking medications for these problems. We hope she will live for a very long time. She has set a fine example for all of us.

5

Getting to Know Patricia Mukamuvara

I would like to tell the story about a remarkable woman survivor. Her name is Patricia Mukamuvara. She was chosen to be the first person to care for the first cow donated to her village. She was a natural leader: the other women respected her. She was also kind, intelligent, and very influential.

We met when I was doing my first training session. She was so happy with our program. The next day she returned on the bus to give me a gift: a small basket she had made. I still treasure this generous gift.

Patricia told me her story. One day during the genocide, she was just walking down a dirt road to her home with her baby on her back. She was attacked, raped, and left in the dirt. When she finally arrived home, she discovered that both her son and her husband had been murdered. Despite these painful losses, she continued to take care of other widows and their children, bringing them into her home when they had no housing.

Years later I was very distressed when Justin wrote to me about Patricia. "I have horrible news." He explained that Patricia was walking down the road, as many others do every day. A truck swerved and hit her, killing her. The entire community came for her funeral, grieved, and talked about what an exceptional person she was. She might be considered "a saint."

6

Working with Trauma Victims

Our intention was to train a number of people who could then teach others how to cope with their trauma from the genocide. We didn't expect very many. We planned for the conference to be held from Monday through Friday in Kigali. Many participants would be walking long distances because they could not afford the bus. Once in Kigali, they would need money for food and lodging. Fortunately, they seemed to have friends with whom they could spend the nights.

My past experiences treating trauma victims in the United States suggested that we focus on three techniques: deep breathing, head-holding, and tapping. I suggested that they start with slow, deep breathing. If individuals felt comfortable, they could tell their own stories of what happened to them during the genocide. Feeling the empathy of the other women would help the speaker tell her story. It could also trigger forgotten memories and many tears.

The second technique was head-holding. One participant would stand behind another, putting one palm on the forehead and the other palm on the back of the neck. Head-holding frequently had a calming effect.

Head-Holding

The third technique was tapping (**Meridian Therapy**). This involved each person gently tapping with their fingertips on meridian pressure-points on the forehead, under the eyes, under the nose, and on the chin.

Our week's work was not limited to breathing, head holding, and tapping. I wanted to create an environment where survivors would be encouraged to talk with others who had had equally hellish experiences. To know that no one was alone could help.

Teaching Tapping

At the end of the training sessions, we offered orange sodas to everyone. This was a special treat for those who could not afford one.

Another method I used was the result of the work of Rita Rivest, a Santa Barbara resident who gave people small boxes to tell their story. I gave boxes to 55 women. They had only limited art materials for this project. Most widows made their boxes into beautiful coffins. They wished they could have given a decent funeral and burial for their husbands who had been murdered and whose bodies just thrown out. The younger girls who were homeless made their boxes into a home with themselves inside. I brought these boxes back to Rita Rivest to add to her collection of boxes from around the world.

Box-making

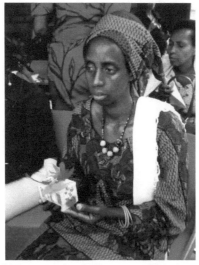
Woman holding coffin box

Staying in our hotel was a Rwandan man who had started a group for widows. Once a week many of these widows would walk miles in their very poor flip flops just to come to a meeting to talk with each other. It was a very effective means of comforting and supporting each other. I was invited to attend a meeting. Even though I didn't have a translator, it was very easy to understand the emotions that were being expressed. The widows talked about their trauma, how they had somehow survived, and now had the courage to carry on. These meetings certainly helped give them the support and strength that they needed. I applied the technique of deep breathing and head holding to some of the women. They were very grateful to learn these techniques which they could share with others.

Typically in Rwanda, word travels very quickly. We were happily surprised to see three pastors and a pastor's wife who had come from the Congo for Bible study. When they heard about our work, they chose to attend our sessions, because they felt it was far more important. After each group session, I would spend extra time with them. They could ask more specific questions. When our training was over, two of these pastors actually had tears in their eyes. "Please come over to Congo with us. We desperately need this help there." Unfortunately, we knew there was not enough time to go over to the Congo to do this same kind of training. Furthermore, because of violent conflicts in eastern Congo at that time, we decided to focus on our unfinished work in Rwanda. I still feel badly that I had to reject their request.

I realized that to reach many people it would be necessary to visit rural communities outside Kigali. That was where most people lived a subsistence life. Traveling to these communities became an important focus after our first visit to Kigali. This took more detailed planning for Justin and me. I needed transportation. Sometimes it took a while to convince the owner of the vehicle that these trips were worthwhile. Sometimes I would even be driven in a vehicle they used as an "ambulance." But anything that got me out there worked. The village would be notified ahead of time. The co-ops are formed by local groups who pool their land and work together, following government-regulated guidelines to equalize work requirements and benefits for the members.

The work I did in the villages was perhaps the most meaningful work I have ever done with people who were in distress. Normally I would visit a co-op for several days but spend each night in Kigali. (I used to hope that I would get invited to spend the night at one of the co-ops. But later I was told that the women were too embarrassed to invite me. They were all sleeping on the ground with a mat of leaves or grass and a cloth.)

We would always start these sessions with deep breathing and then teach other techniques. At one co-op a woman giggled and said, "Oh, but I know how to breathe!" When we would travel further away from the Kigali, Justin always knew where we could stay. We would stay at a modest hostel that would be both clean and safe. There was one I particularly enjoyed. Run by the Anglican church, the hostel overlooked a very beautiful lake. The cook provided a good meal. This evening was a brief but lovely respite.

Usually every woman in the village was very eager to sit with us in a group and talk. We would sit in a circle. Some of the women would stand up and tell their story of what had happened to them. Justin would translate for me. Hearing a trembling voice and seeing a sad person often crying made it clear that they were talking about terrible abuse. The speaker, however, would feel the strong support of the group. No doubt they had told their story to close friends but having the group meetings seemed to be very effective. We would always end our final co-op meeting with a celebration. This consisted of having a soft drink brought for everyone — one for each of them so that no one had to share. It was a wonderful way to end our work. There were always many hugs and often tears when we said goodbye.

In one village there were more women than usual, but we followed the same pattern of everyone sitting in a circle while those who wanted to talk told their story. I shall never be able to forget this incident. When the killers came, they took a woman's little boy and pulled him up to his father. They killed the father while the mother watched. The leader then poured gasoline on the child and threw a match at him. He would burn to death, as no one tried to save him. Her friends in the circle had heard this story before but still cried. How can one not cry when you hear of this kind of cruelty? I was amazed at the strength and bravery of this mother.

As Justin and I were saying goodbye to these widows, a woman came up with tears in her eyes and three children at her side. She had just been told that she had to move out of her house immediately because she could not pay any rent. Her friends gathered around her in sympathy. They tried to think of an alternative shelter for that night. One woman knew a gardening hut that had some tools in it. "Let's move the tools so that the mother and her children would be able to lie down on the grass." It was hard leaving this situation knowing the dire straits she was in.

It could be very hard to get to these faraway villages because trucks and vans were not plentiful. However, we did hear about a group of widows who had really suffered unbelievably during the genocide. We were able to secure an ambulance.

As we drove into the village, we crossed a rickety wooden bridge over a river. Later in the session, a woman told me her story about that river. She and another woman ran to the river when the killers came. They hid in tall grass by the river. This incident occurred during the rainy season. If necessary, the women could duck under the water to hide. The woman was trembling as she continued. They had had nothing to eat. They did not dare leave their hiding place, as the killers were still walking around the area. On the night of the third day, her friend had died. On the fourth day, she was so hungry she started to eat her dead friend. She had tears in her eyes when telling her story. Perhaps she needed to make what she felt was a confession. She was so hungry she did not know what else to do. The hunger simply overwhelmed her. I think that she had never told anybody about this before. She felt so ashamed, but she wanted to tell me. She probably reasoned that it would be helpful to "confess" to a person who would not tell other residents. After this experience, whenever I crossed this bridge, I would think about this young woman.

After my return from the 5th trip to Rwanda, I became seriously ill. I lost 30 pounds. It was even difficult to get out of bed. My travel doctor tried every possible diagnostic test. She even sent specimens to the Menninger Clinic. We assumed it had to be some kind of African bug, but all these tests revealed nothing.

Fortunately, I slowly recovered. I regained my appetite and started to think about my next trip to Rwanda. Understandably David was reluctant to have me return to Rwanda. But I was convinced I had to return, as there was still work to be done.

Altogether, I made nine trips to Rwanda between 2006 and 2014, usually staying for three weeks. But my involvement with fundraising for Rwanda continues to this day.

7

Forgiveness and Reconciliation

The personal stories about the genocide horrified me. Instances of mass killings were even more appalling. For example, it was assumed that taking haven in a church or school would protect you, as had been the case in previous genocides. This, however, was not the case in 1994. A priest in a Catholic Church in Kigali urged Tutsis into his church for safety. The doors were locked so that no one could enter or escape. Maybe the terrified Tutsis assumed that locking the doors would prevent the mob from entering. Instead, the church was set ablaze. In another instance, Tutsis gathered at a "safe" church. Once they were safely inside, the mob brought in bulldozers to level the church. No Tutsis survived.

I know of one instance at a teaching hospital where a Tutsi went for help. The Hutu physician asked to see his identity card. When he saw that the patient was a Tutsi, he walked out of the room and refused to treat him.

There were other Rwandans who did risk injury or even death to help the terrified Tutsis. I heard directly from the sister of a Tutsi woman who was about to have a baby. Her Hutu physician risked his life to deliver the baby.

Rwandan courts and jails were unable to deal with so many cases. The jails were already so overcrowded that only those responsible for more than 100 deaths were jailed. Communities had to create their own justice system to deal with the genocide. In the countryside, many formed gacacas (courts) where people would sit on the ground, hear the horrifying details of torture and death, and pass judgment on the accused.

Many prisoners, when released, returned to their village. In our co-ops, a Methodist pastor and Justin asked the surviving family members how they would feel working with the released killers, raising livestock, and helping widows in everyday living. There is preliminary evidence that some widows have been willing to forgive. Young people also tell me that they have a song they sing in groups. "We are working together, and we will build back our country." Let us hope that this effort to forgive will continue to make progress.

8

Gifting Goats and Cows

We knew that better nutrition was extremely important for the families living on a subsistence income. David and I believed that to get at least one cow for every village and a goat for each family in that village were worthy goals. Our initial emphasis would be goats. They were relatively inexpensive and easy to transport from the market to the co-op. We named our effort *Goats for Gifts* (later changed to *Goats for Life*). Between 2007 and 2010, we sent 2,550 goats ($45 each) and 20 cows (a minimum cost of $1,000 each).

We also knew that having a registered nonprofit organization (501c3) would make donors more comfortable giving to our effort. Getting a 501c3 designation took some effort and time, but we were sure that it helped us raise approximately $500,000.

We announced that all contributions would go directly to Rwanda; no money was used for overhead. The office was our dining room table; transportation costs, mailings, and a few gatherings to advertise our efforts were under-written by us or close friends. Our efforts would not have succeeded without the generosity of our donors.

Goats

Goats can contribute in many ways to the well-being and economic prosperity of the family. Goats can give birth twice a year and often have twins. They can be pets for the children. In addition, their manure is a very rich fertilizer; crops will grow more abundantly. Baby goats can be sold for much-needed cash.

One of the first recipients of a goat was woman who had suffered extreme mistreatment during the genocide. She was now limping, blinded in one eye, and had head-burns from a house-fire. So a goat was an ideal animal for her. She was so thrilled with what this goat was doing and what it meant to her. When I visited, she grabbed my arm, and pulled me over to meet her goat and to see her very lush, abundant garden. It was clear that giving livestock was worthwhile.

We delivered goats to two villages that had been totally burned down. The widows were ecstatic that goats were arriving. But first they had to listen to a long speech by the woman in charge with instructions on how to care for the goats. I still have a photo of these women sitting under a very large tree in the shade while the woman was giving her talk; they were either under umbrellas or leaning forward eager to hear every word.

During the talk, a truck had delivered the goats to a large field. When the talk was over, we walked to the field. Arrival of the goats was a moment of great excitement and joy.

Each new owner gladly signed a contract promising to take good care of their goat.

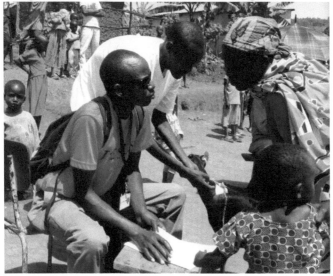

Cows

We wanted mature cows for our co-ops. They would be more expensive, but they would give milk immediately. Some organizations only give very young calves. The recipients must wait years before their calf can produce milk.

When the cows arrived in the village, a veterinarian would discuss various aspects of cow care, including medical issues as well as the best milking techniques. The women (It was almost always women; few men survived the genocide.) would be attentive and take very good notes. They were also asked to sign a contract stating that they would take good care of the animal. The milk and cheese from the cow would probably feed several families.

The arrival of a cow would ignite a wonderful celebration. Often there would be dancing around the cow, clapping, and making joyful noises to celebrate the arrival.

They had the official "introduction" of their new cow for me. They would milk the cow and then pour the milk into a very large cup. The cup was passed around the circle. Each person would drink some milk before passing to the next person. I also drank from the cup without any concern about germs.

(Photo courtesy of World Dance for Humanity)

Justin and I also spent time visiting one very large slum in Kigali. I was appalled to see muddy water running through the slum where people did their laundry. There was no alternative.

Justin and I were trying to determine what would be needed to have more productive gardens in this area. After my third or fourth visit, a friendly local Rwandan official became very curious. "What are you doing? Why do you keep coming back?" I explained. He invited me to his office to have more discussion. His English was excellent. There was a sign on his desk. "The most efficient way to remove poverty is the giving of livestock." I told him about our goat and cow program for co-ops. He heartily approved.

9

The Kungabu Fish Farm

Our most complex but rewarding project was the successful development of the Kungabu Fish Farm. The farm is located in the southwestern part of Rwanda and very near Lake Kivu. Before the farm was completed, the co-op workers had few employment opportunities. Many were picking tea leaves for an Indian company for a subsistence wage and long hours.

One elderly man thought we should consider fish farming. We had a willing labor **force** and plenty of water nearby. Furthermore, there was an upscale resort nearby to provide a market for our product. In 2008, everyone in the village started to dig sixteen large ponds for the fish.

Many people provided generous financial support for this project. A Santa Barbara realtor, Linda Lorenzen-Hughes, honored her late husband Bill Hughes by underwriting the training of a co-op member in fish husbandry.

(Photo courtesy of Justin Bisengimana)

Our biggest expense was the purchase and delivery of a fish-food machine. Without this machine, we had to rely on fish food from Uganda which was a very expensive source.

The fish-food machine was built in China, but Justin was able to get government approval to waive any import fees. We still needed to raise $27,500 for the machine from skeptical donors. My dermatologist's 12-year-old daughter, Sadie

40

Leventhal, used her bat mitzvah gift of $4,350 to finally reach our necessary financial needs. Men and women in the village were so impressed by her generosity that they made and sent her a very intricate and beautifully carved fish **platter**.

Sadie Leventhal
(Photo courtesy of Rebecca Miller)

When the fish-food machine arrived in Rwanda, the government tried to put duty tariffs on the machine. But Justin successfully reminded them of their previous promise of no import duties. Then we had to get it on a truck to transport it down to the southern part of the country. The bottom line is that it has been an enormous success. Besides being able to make their own fish food, they now sell to other fish farmers in the area. A happy surprise was that this machine will also grind up wheat and other grasses that are needed.

On a later visit to the fish farm, I was invited to join in the wonderful, happy celebration of the great success they were having. We walked a-round each pond singing while someone beat a drum. I really enjoyed joining in the celebration and sharing the great happiness of these wonder-ful, hard-working people.

(Photo courtesy of Harriet Eckstein)

One added bonus of this happy celebration: when a friend of ours saw me in the video dancing around the fishponds, he said, "Well, I think I need to give you a generous donation for this." My first, and probably my only, donation from a dance!

A girlfriend of mine from Santa Barbara who had gone with me realized how very close the Congo was to this fish farm. She was very eager to walk over at least to the border of Congo and see what she could see. I too had been very curious after all my trips that close to Congo, so I let her talk me into it. We proceeded across the border and immediately the border guards demanded that we show our passports. (Wow, was I scared!) We explained we were just tourists and had come only for a very short time. But it became increasingly clear this was a very foolish thing to do. These guards were probably just having a good time scaring us, I think. Fortunately, we were able to get out before too long, but it is a memory that has certainly stayed in my head.

10

Fundraising

Raising money was the most difficult part of the project. We talked to family and friends about Rwanda. I think they understood the plight of the Rwandans but were focused on more local projects sponsored by churches, colleges, and local or national nonprofits. Some of the parishioners at All Saints-by-the-Sea Episcopal Church in Santa Barbara understood the need. The church raised sufficient money to buy goats and three mature cows in Rwanda for our villages.

The rector encouraged us to continue the project, but we knew this was going to be difficult. There would always be people who felt that money sent to a small nation in Africa would be wasted. Numerous cases would be cited to support their position. We did not waste time trying to persuade them that our project would have better results. We knew that we would need to get good, trust-worthy people for our project. This was especially true for our contacts in Rwanda who would be needed for the important day-to-day management of our project.

Our initial fund-raising efforts were basically discussions with individuals who we thought would be interested in providing some support. Every coffee hour after the sermon we would talk about our plans for Rwanda. I think it helped a great deal that an accountant, Kent Englert, willingly did all of the accounting work gratis for several years. This included sending a letter acknowledging and thanking donors for their gift as well as a tax letter each year for IRS purposes. A yearly list of the donors was also made available to us.

A small group of women heard about the project and got involved. They invited me to join them. They even organized a recital with some of the best local musicians. All the admission money went towards our work. Husbands were all also helpful sending emails and writing letters. One women's church held a "potluck" lunch to raise money for Rwanda. Another small church held a luncheon event specifically to raise money for our work. We thanked them with a beautiful painting from Rwanda. They hung this painting in their sanctuary. This support reassured us that the project would be worthwhile. More hard work might be necessary, but the chance of success seemed to improve with this kind of support.

Other generous donors in Santa Barbara stepped forward in specific hours of need. For example, Justin had introduced me to two of his younger friends and their mother. They lived in the Kigali slums. The husband had been murdered during the genocide. The mother was working in construction to support the family. She then suffered a broken leg from an industrial accident. There was no insurance, no pain medication, and no job to support her family! She ultimately died with no support for her children. I asked a Santa Barbara couple if they could help. Their support gave these children food and financed their schooling. Eventually the older daughter went to bakery school and got a job working as a baker's assistant. The boy is doing much better as well.

Some wealthy people have been very generous in supporting our work, but I am especially moved when the less fortunate want to give as well. One man living out of his car insisted on giving us a few dollars to help. He said, "I know what it's like to be homeless."

11

Clean-Water Filtration Project

Another important initiative was bringing a new clean drinking-water resource to our co-operatives. Local donors in Santa Barbara, Harriet Eckstein and Alan Irwin, who used their own funds to visit Rwanda with me in November of 2014, saw for themselves the effects of drinking impure water; the vast distances that people traveled—usually on foot—to fetch clean water; and the hours spent boiling water to make it potable. Thanks to them, the Clean Water Ambassador Foundation initiated a program for supplying water filters to eight of the co-ops.

Harriet describes some of the program's history here:

PILOT PROGRAM

In 2014, Harriet Eckstein and Alan Irwin, Clean Water Ambassador Foundation (CWAF – http://cleanwaterambassadors.org/) ambassadors, introduced CWAF to Justin Bisengimana and conducted the first five water filter training programs at co-operatives supported by World Dance for Humanity (WD4H).

STAFFING & COORDINATION

The initial water filter training/distribution program was deemed a success, and in 2016, Harriet and Alan returned to Rwanda with several dozen water filters and conducted additional trainings. At that time, they connected with local Kigali CWAF ambassador Clément Mugisha in order to assess his availability to do future culturally appropriate trainings in conjunction with Justin and the African Blessings staff. Having been introduced to Clément, Justin proceeded to develop a more comprehensive training and distribution plan.

(Photo courtesy of Harriet Eckstein)

TRAINING & DISTRIBUTION

A key feature of the distribution plan is that, prior to receiving the water filters, co-op members decide collectively where the filters will be situated, with families or at centralized locations (i.e., health center; church; community gathering place). For example, one family might be responsible for securing and maintaining a system that is shared with three or four nearby families. Training includes the principles behind the Sawyer portable water filters, assembly/installation, use, and maintenance. In 2019, Clean Water Ambassador Foundation donated an additional 200 water filters, each of which provides clean water for 10 people for approximately three years. WD4H staff brought the filters to Rwanda where CWAF ambassador Clément Mugisha conducted the trainings along with Program Director Justin Bisengimana and assistance from WD4H volunteer Allison O'Brien.

(Photo courtesy of Harriet Eckstein)

WD4H generously provided additional funding to pay for 200 large buckets, a stipend to Clément, and transportation costs for the team.

Harriet kindly also supplied a description of their experience as donors:

"Alan and I were often nearly speechless and overwhelmed by the welcomes and gifts we received at co-op after co-op. Of course we were thanked for being donors and bringing water filters, but we sensed that we were appreciated even more for simply being there, for witnessing, for acknowledging a people who had been abandoned by the world. And, after all, we were with Betsy, without whom, none of these water initiatives would have existed. Without a doubt, the bond they feel with her and their love for her were, and continue to be, boundless. To accompany Betsy was to experience a master class in grace, humbleness, eloquence, encouragement, and openness.

Betsy's work, quite literally, saved lives and it created the means for a future for generations of Rwandans. It was a profound honor to be a tiny bit of her massive, heartfelt endeavor."

World Dance for Humanity

In 2013 David and I turned the *Goats for Life* organization over to World Dance for Humanity (https://worlddanceforhumanity.org/current-projects-2/) a nonprofit based in Santa Barbara. I actively support these efforts and help with fundraising wherever possible. The director of this nonprofit, Janet Reineck, has continued and expanded our work and upheld our policy of directing 100% of every donation designated to Rwanda to the work there — not a penny to overhead.

Betsy with Janet Reineck

WD4H Team (L to R): Dany Rukundo, Janet Reineck, Chantal Kubwimana, Justin Bisengimana, Judy Rwibutso, and Genevieve Feiner
(Photos courtesy of World Dance for Humanity)

To date (February 2023), WD4H has made so many significant contributions to Rwanda, building on our initiatives, including the following (listed on their website):

- 1,576 goats for families
- 83 full-grown, pregnant cows collectively owned by the co-op (including 19 cows soon to be delivered)
- 111 calves from these cows
- 7 parcels of farmland
- Education stipends for 390 primary, high school, and college students

- Two preschools for children 4-7 years-old, including buildings, equipment, and teachers' salaries
- Annual training workshops in agriculture, veterinary, business, and leadership
- Health insurance for 955 people (on average) each year who cannot afford the $5 annual fee
- 19 co-op businesses: bakeries, seamstresses, event rentals, a water project, a café, ventilation bricks, a craft store, bees, beet-juice, and a tilapia fish farm
- Reusable menstrual pad production in 4 co-ops
- 400 water filters & training
- 35 bicycles for businesses to transport goods
- 613 mattresses
- 619 solar lights
- 66 clean-air cookstoves
- 8 laptops to co-op businesses
- 6 rainwater collection tanks

A recent bequest of $148,000 from Renate Bellville to WD4H will ensure the continuation of World Dance for Humanity's work far into the future. The policy of not spending donations on overhead had attracted Renate to give to our work, as it probably did with many other donors.

I continue to stay in touch with Justin and to encourage donations to Rwanda. To my great sorrow, I can no longer visit there for health reasons. But my long association with the country has left a lasting impression on me and an enduring compassion for the suffering of these resilient people, who set a great example for finding strength despite adversity.

Practical Suggestions for Traveling or Working in Rwanda; Bibliography

Travel Tips

- Be sure to start getting your travel shots well in advance and collect all the medicine you are going to need to take with you to Rwanda, including whatever a travel doctor suggests.
- Make sure you have sunscreen and all prescribed medications. There is very little chance that you will be able to duplicate your medications in Rwanda.
- You do not want to get malaria. Do all that you possibly can by putting on anti-malarial spray during the day. At night be very careful when you pull down your mosquito net. Make sure there are no mosquitoes hiding in the folds of the net.
- Avoid the rainy season, if possible. Rain can slow traffic. If you have room in your suitcase, take your own rain gear. Downpours

do sometimes occur outside of the rainy season.

- Write a daily diary. I regret very much that I did not write in mine every night as I had planned to. However, I was so tired I usually just immediately went to sleep. But you could work around that and even write in your diary during the day perhaps.
- Ask your host the most cost-effective way to exchange money.

Courtesy Suggestions

- ***Prior to going to Rwanda to do charity work or aid projects, ask Rwandans for their opinion about the project. Do not assume you know what they most need. Throughout your project, be very conscious and listen very carefully to what the Rwandans say.
- If you want to help people with construction and painting of buildings, please consider sending the money over there for them to do it rather than volunteering your labor. There are Rwandan carpenters and construction workers who are very capable. People are desperate for jobs; there are many, many people looking for work all the time. If they are offered the materials, they will be able to work for themselves and start their own businesses. For example, during my last trip to Rwanda, I heard of some older adoles-

cent boys who had learned how to do brickmaking and bricklaying. However, they did not have the money to start their own bricklaying business. If they only had had some start-up money, they could have had a very successful business.

- If you are going to Rwanda because you know a missionary family or aid worker who lives in Kigali, please invite them out rather than having them invite you to dinner. Missionaries often feel they need to entertain people coming from their home area. However, they are very busy doing their own work and taking care of their own children. It would be such a treat if you could take them out to dinner.

- Ask missionaries or aid workers what medications or other items they might need.

- Take small gifts for people you meet (e.g., ball-point pens, razors, or colorful head scarves).

- Always ask permission before taking someone's photo.

- Almost every village you visit will probably have some memorial to those killed during the 1994 genocide. If you find this too stressful, ask politely if you can be excused. Do not simply leave.

Select Bibliography

Daillaire, Roméo. 2004. *Shake Hands with the Devil. The Failure of Humanity in Rwanda.* Boston: Da Capo Press.

Gourevitch, Philip. 1999. *We Wish to Inform You That Tomorrow We Will Be Killed with Our Families: Stories from Rwanda.* New York: Picador.

Hatzfeld, Jean. 2006. *Machete Season: The Killers in Rwanda Speak.* Translated by Linda Coverdale. New York: Picador.

Hatzfeld, Jean. 2007. *Life Laid Bare: The Survivors in Rwanda Speak.* New York: Other Press.

Hatzfeld,Jean. 2010. *The Antelope's Strategy: Living in Rwanda after the Genocide.* New York: Picador.

Appendix: Tanzania (2013)

According to a January 11, 2017, report written by Kathryn Hanlon for The Organization for World Peace (Female Genital Mutilation In Tanzania – The Organization for World Peace (theowp.org), Female Genital Mutilation (FGM) is a practice that involves the complete or partial removal or alteration of the genitalia for non-medical reasons. It is usually performed by an elderly woman, a position of respect in the village and often her main source of income.

FGM has become ingrained in Tanzanian society because some believe that:

- FGM can protect a girl's virginity, the family's honor and secure a suitable marriage
- It is a rite of passage
- It can help to control a girl's sex drive
- It enhances male sexual pleasure

The World Health Organization (WHO) in 2013 determined that 10-25% of girls and women aged 15-49 in Tanzania (7.9 million) had undergone FGM. Since 1998, the Sexual Offences Special Provisions Act outlaws FGM on girls under the age of 18, but enforcement is weak, and the Act does not protect girls over that age.

In 2013, I went to Tanzania to visit a co-ed school which included girls who were there primarily to escape female genital mutilation but also to get an education. Many modern mothers were helping their daughters to avoid this procedure in their villages by placing them in such schools.

When I first arrived by a small plane, I was detained by the one customs official while the other two passengers were waved through with no inspection. He pulled out each item in my suitcase slowly, clearly hoping for a bribe. I was not about to give him money. After about 20 minutes, suddenly a very tall Tanzanian man in full local dress walked up to the customs official and asked, "Where is the passenger I've been waiting for?" Immediately the customs official returned everything to the suitcase and handed it to me. The driver had come to take me to the school.

It was a fascinating and long ride with this gentleman. We rode through very heavy tall brush on our way to the school. At one point he stopped and pointed out to me, waving his hand across the road, "And a large elephant has clearly just walked across our path." I have often wondered what would have happened if indeed we had met that large elephant as he crossed our path. We were clearly moving very deeply into the region where the school was located.

My purpose in going to this school was because I was considering giving them goats to help fund their operation, as we had done in **Rwanda**, and I always visited a facility before we gave goats to be sure that they were in need of funding.

Faculty and students lived very modestly at the school. The teachers had very primitive iron beds with just a thin mattress and a roof to protect against rain. The "toilet" was a large hole in the ground not far from the sleeping area. It appeared that they were served only two meals of soup a day, one at lunch and one in the evening. Electricity and water were only available sporadically. I very much admired the dedication of the teachers who were living this extremely simple, even primitive, life. They probably could have gotten much easier, better-paying jobs elsewhere.

I spent my first day talking with the girls, with someone there to translate when necessary. They were very interested in life in America as well as telling me about their lives at the school. The boys especially were thrilled that I had brought some music from America. To my surprise they seemed to know many of the current popular songs in the U.S.A It appeared that they did get radio several hours a day, so this is probably how they got that music as well as news. Before the evening soup, the boys demonstrated their abilities at jumping straight into the air, quite high, to my amazement! I assume they must have been taught from childhood to do this.

Before I left, several of the women dressed me in their beautiful ceremonial clothes. We laughed and giggled and had a wonderful time. This was great fun for me.

At the end of this visit, I determined that they were clearly entitled to receive some goats. They would be a great source of income for this community. Probably for the rest of my life I shall continue to hold my respect, fondness, and admiration for the teachers and the students at this school. It was a privilege to be there.

Acknowledgements

My greatest debt is to my husband David for his constant support for my work in Rwanda. Henry and Rebecca Tinsley generously financed our first trip to Rwanda and introduced me to the country and people who would come to mean so much to me. I would also like to thank Nancy Winter for encouraging me to write my memoirs of Rwanda, for finding the dictation software to make creating a text relatively easy, and for discussing with me the scope of the story and individual stories prior to dictation. She also helped edit the final text, insert the photographs, and do the layout and uploading process for publication. Harriet Eckstein graciously provided text and photographs for the clean-water filter chapter. My *Goats for Life* successor, Janet Reineck, executive director of World Dance for Humanity, kindly provided some names, dates, photographs, and statistics for this book. Craig Smith, Nancy Smith, and John Balkwill generously helped with design and production expertise. Too many people to thank individually contributed in other ways. Last but not least, my utmost thanks go to all the generous donors who helped so much to improve the lives of traumatized and impoverished Rwandans.

All photographs, except where otherwise credited, are my own.

All profits from the sale of this book will go to World Dance for Humanities for their continuing work in Rwanda.

CPSIA information can be obtained
at www.ICGtesting.com
Printed in the USA
LVHW071939280423
745592LV00001B/3